Who Was?

WORKBOOK

GRADE 3
Science/Social Studies

Based on the #1 *New York Times* Best-Selling Who Was? Series

Mini-biographies with maps, diagrams, timelines, and graphic organizers, plus puzzles, word searches, and tons of fun!

written by Linda Ross

PENGUIN WORKSHOP
An Imprint of Penguin Random House LLC, New York

Penguin supports copyright. Copyright fuels creativity, encourages diverse voices, promotes free speech, and creates a vibrant culture. Thank you for buying an authorized edition of this book and for complying with copyright laws by not reproducing, scanning, or distributing any part of it in any form without permission. You are supporting writers and allowing Penguin to continue to publish books for every reader.

Cover illustrations by Nancy Harrison
Interior illustrations by Nancy Harrison, Mattia Cerato, Gary LaCoste, Scott MacNeill, and Chris Vallo

Photo credits: p. 30 Courtesy of Ford Motor Company; p. 37 Fred Schilling, Collection of the Supreme Court of the United States

Designed by Dinardo Design

Visit us online at www.penguinrandomhouse.com.

ISBN 9780593225776   10 9 8 7 6 5 4 3 2 1

Who Was?
WORKBOOK

INSTRUCTIONS

Welcome to the wonderful world of Who Was?, filled with the greatest people in science and history. This workbook is packed with fascinating fact-filled passages about people you'll want to learn about. It also has fun activities that will help you apply the information you learn in new and exciting ways. Here's what you'll find:

Just for Fun! pages contain crossword puzzles, word searches, mazes, crack-the-code pages, and more!

Read and Annotate pages are loaded with interesting information about famous people in science and history. Mark up the passages as you read to help you better remember the facts. You can circle, underline, draw, and add notes.

Show What You Know pages show how much you learned. You'll use maps, diagrams, photos, timelines, and all kinds of charts. So, show off!

Vocabulary Connection pages help you learn the meanings of science and social studies words and terms. You'll want to impress your friends!

Writing Connection pages give you space to be creative and write opinions, explanations, and descriptions that connect what you read to your life.

LAUGH OUT LOUD!

Write the answer to each joke. Use the answer choices in the box on the next page.

What did the sheep say when he saw President Obama?

_____

Why were Betsy Ross's feet tired?

_____

When did Abraham Lincoln make meatballs?

_____

Why did Michelle Obama win the marathon?

_____

Why do cows like Neil Armstrong?

_____

Why did Thomas Edison read so much about electricity?

_____

Why was Sally Ride so hungry?

_____

Why did Orville and Wilbur Wright like to stay inside?

_____

Why did Amelia Earhart want to fly around the world?

_____

What did Ben Franklin say after discovering that lightning was electricity?

_____

Answer Choices

"I am _shocked_!"

Because he liked _current_ events!

Because life at home was too _plane_!

Because she forgot to eat her _launch_!

During the _Spaghetti_-sburg Address!

Because she was the _First Lady_ to cross the finish line!

Because they were _in_-ventors!

Because of her American indepen-_dance_!

Because he was the first man on the _moooooo_-n!

"Hi, _Baaaaa_-rack!"

AN IMPORTANT MESSENGER
Paul Revere

As you read:

- Underline important words
- Circle confusing words or sentences
- Add drawings or notes to remember important facts

NOTES

By the 1770s, many Americans wanted to break away from England to start a new country. Paul Revere was one of them. He had an important role. He was a messenger who spread the news about the Revolution.

Paul was a skilled silversmith. He had a big family. He also belonged to a secret group. It was called the Sons of Liberty. This group was against paying taxes to the British.

In 1773, Paul took part in the Boston Tea Party. The men sneaked aboard British ships. They dumped chests of tea into the harbor. Why? If no one bought the tea, no taxes could be paid on it!

Paul spread the news about the Boston Tea Party. He rode his horse to New York City and Philadelphia. The trip took 11 days. This was the first of many rides.

On April 18, 1775, Paul made his famous ride to Lexington. He warned that British troops were on their way. Thanks to Paul, the people of Lexington were ready for them. Indeed, on the next day, the American Revolution began.

FIND THE FACTS

Use the map to answer questions 1-2. Use the passage about Paul Revere to answer questions 3-5.

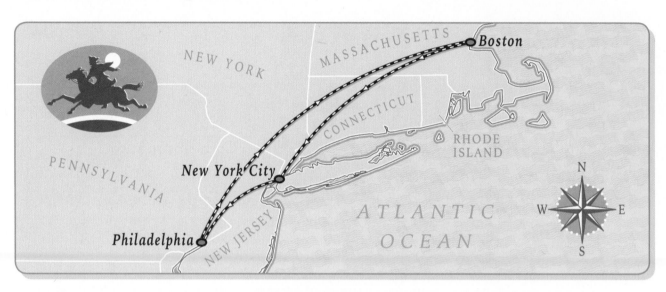

1. Which city is farther from Boston—New York City or Philadelphia?

_____

2. In what direction was Paul Revere traveling when he rode to these cities?

_____

3. What role did Paul play in the American Revolution?

_____

_____

4. What secret group did Paul belong to?

_____

5. What was the purpose of the Boston Tea Party?

_____

_____

THEN AND NOW

Paul Revere traveled by horseback to share important news. Fill in the chart to show the different ways people may have traveled and communicated in colonial times and the different ways people travel and communicate now.

Then	
Travel	**Communication**

Now	
Travel	**Communication**

Tell about some of the ways that you travel and communicate with your family and friends.

_____

_____

_____

_____

QUIET COURAGE
Rosa Parks

As you read:

- Underline important words
- Circle confusing words or sentences
- Add drawings or notes to remember important facts

NOTES

_____

_____

_____

_____

_____

_____

_____

_____

Rosa Parks grew up in Alabama. At that time in the South, Black people and white people led separate lives. Black children and white children went to separate schools.

Rosa enjoyed school. But after she started high school, she had to drop out. Why? She had to take care of her sick grandmother. It wasn't until after she married that she finished high school.

Rosa and her husband moved to Montgomery, Alabama. There she became active in the Civil Rights Movement. Rosa joined the NAACP (National Association for the

Advancement of Colored People). It is the oldest civil rights group in the U.S.

In 1955, Rosa was working in a department store. Each day, she rode the bus to and from work. One day, the bus driver told her to give up her seat for a white person. Rosa would not get up. She was arrested!

Rosa's arrest led to a bus boycott. Black people stopped riding the buses for over a year. Then in 1956, the boycott ended. There would be no more "whites only" seats on buses. It was Rosa's quiet courage that sparked the change.

USE A TIMELINE

Use the timeline below and the passage about Rosa Parks to answer the questions on the next page.

Timeline of Rosa Parks's Life

1913 Born in Tuskegee, Alabama

1924 Enrolls in Montgomery Industrial School for Girls

1932 Marries Raymond Parks

1934 Receives high school diploma

1943 Becomes secretary of the Montgomery chapter of the NAACP

1944 Works at Maxwell Air Force Base

1945 Registers to vote

1955 Is arrested for refusing to give her bus seat to a white person on December 1; Montgomery Bus Boycott starts

1956 Montgomery Bus Boycott ends

1957 Moves to Detroit, Michigan

1965 Begins working for Rep. John Conyers, Jr., of Michigan

1977 Raymond Parks dies

1987 Establishes the Rosa and Raymond Parks Institute for Self Development

1988 Retires after more than twenty years in Conyers's office

1992 Publishes her first book, *Rosa Parks: My Story*, with Jim Haskins

1996 Receives the highest U.S. civilian honor, the Presidential Medal of Freedom

1999 Awarded the Congressional Gold Medal of Honor

2005 Dies at 92

QUESTIONS

1. Where and when was Rosa Parks born?

   _____

   _____

2. When did Rosa receive her high school diploma? Why did it take so long?

   _____

   _____

   _____

3. What role did Rosa have in the NAACP?

   _____

   _____

4. Rosa's refusal to give up her seat on the bus had big effects. What were they?

   _____

   _____

   _____

5. What honors did Rosa receive?

   _____

   _____

6. What impressed you the most about Rosa Parks?

   _____

   _____

AN INVENTOR WHO CHANGED OUR WORLD
Thomas Alva Edison

As you read:

- Underline important words
- Circle confusing words or sentences
- Add drawings or notes to remember important facts

NOTES

_____

_____

_____

_____

_____

_____

_____

_____

The world was very different in 1847 when Thomas Alva Edison was born. There were no electric lights or movies. There was no recorded music. Thomas made all these things possible and much more. He changed our world.

In 1876, Thomas had his own company in Menlo Park, New Jersey. It was where he invented the phonograph. What did that machine do? It recorded sound and played it back! Thomas became known as "The Wizard of Menlo Park."

His next invention made him even more famous. Thomas began working on a lightbulb that would last a long time. He worked hard on the lightbulb with his team. At last, on October 22, 1879, his lightbulb glowed for 13½ hours. The next one glowed for over 100 hours. The long-lasting lightbulb was born!

Later on, Thomas became interested in moving pictures. He came up with a system to film and show them. His *kinetograph* was the camera. It took the pictures. His *kinetoscope* provided a way to look at the moving pictures.

Thomas Alva Edison's inventions changed our lives forever. Can you even imagine a world without them?

NOTES

TARGET SCIENCE VOCABULARY

Choose the word from the word bank that completes each sentence.

Word Bank

kinetograph	lightbulb	sound
phonograph	invention	kinetoscope

1. Anything that can be heard can be called a _____.

2. A _____ has a glass covering and produces light from an electric current.

3. A machine that records and plays back sounds is a _____.

4. People used a _____ to view early movies, or moving pictures.

5. When people make or design something that didn't exist before, they create a new _____.

6. The _____ was a kind of camera for taking a series of moving pictures.

What does it mean to be an **inventor**? Define the word, and tell what traits an inventor would probably have.

_____

_____

_____

THREE IMPORTANT INVENTIONS

The passage you just read focused on three of Thomas Edison's important inventions. In your own words, write something you learned about each invention.

phonograph

long-lasting lightbulb

kinetograph

Now write down some of the different ways electric lights are used (inside and outside) today.

_____

_____

_____

GREAT SCIENTISTS

Read about some great scientists and their achievements.
Then find the **bold-faced** words in the word search.

P	H	N	C	A	E	B	C	N	A	L	R
P	E	S	T	I	C	I	D	E	S	W	D
Y	T	V	N	Q	D	F	B	S	T	N	X
C	N	I	J	R	V	O	Z	K	R	M	R
H	Q	K	V	A	H	C	S	M	O	O	N
I	R	P	A	D	J	A	F	G	N	C	B
M	K	F	B	I	T	L	H	R	A	X	F
P	E	A	N	U	T	S	T	D	U	V	K
S	X	L	A	M	P	E	Y	B	T	U	H

Jane Goodall lived among the **chimps** and studied their habits.

As commander of Apollo 11, Neil Armstrong was the first man on the **moon**.

Ben Franklin invented a new kind of eyeglasses, called **bifocals**.

George Washington Carver developed hundreds of products that could be made from **peanuts**.

Rachel Carson wrote about the dangers of **pesticides**, which are chemicals sprayed on crops.

Sally Ride was the first American female **astronaut** to fly in space.

Marie Curie discovered the chemical element called **radium**.

Jane Goodall

George Washington Carver

Marie Curie

CRACK THE CODE

Crack the code to find answers to questions about famous people in history.

A	B	C	D	E	F	G	H	I	J	K	L	M
1	2	3	4	5	6	7	8	9	10	11	12	13

N	O	P	Q	R	S	T	U	V	W	X	Y	Z
14	15	16	17	18	19	20	21	22	23	24	25	26

1. **Who made an 11,000-mile trip from Venice, Italy, to China and back?**

___ ___ ___ ___ ___   ___ ___ ___ ___
13 1 18 3 15   16 15 12 15

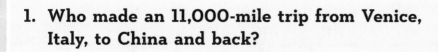

2. **Who fought for a woman's right to vote?**

___ ___ ___ ___ ___ ___. ___ ___ ___ ___ ___ ___ ___
19 21 19 1 14   2   1 14 20 8 15 14 25

3. **Who was the first Black president of South Africa?**

___ ___ ___ ___ ___ ___ ___ ___ ___ ___ ___ ___ ___
14 5 12 19 15 14   13 1 14 4 5 12 1

4. **Who helped Lewis and Clark travel across the American Northwest?**

___ ___ ___ ___ ___ ___ ___ ___ ___
19 1 3 1 7 1 23 5 1

5. **Who signed the Declaration of Independence and was a U.S. president?**

___ ___ ___ ___ ___ ___ ___ ___ ___ ___ ___ ___ ___ ___ ___
20 8 15 13 1 19   10 5 6 6 5 18 19 15 14

SHE CARED ABOUT OUR PLANET
Rachel Carson

As you read:

- Underline important words
- Circle confusing words or sentences
- Add drawings or notes to remember important facts

NOTES

_____

_____

_____

_____

_____

_____

_____

_____

_____

_____

Rachel Carson was born on a farm in Pennsylvania in 1907. Growing up, she learned to love nature. At college, she decided to become a scientist. Later on, she worked for the U.S. Fish and Wildlife Service. She also began writing articles and books about the sea. Those books became best sellers! After that, Rachel left her job to spend all her time writing. She wanted to write about the natural world that she loved so much.

For her next book, Rachel did research on pesticides. These chemicals were sprayed on crops and plants to kill insects. In her book, Rachel explained how harmful they were. Insects and other animals that ate the sprayed plants got sick. Some of them died. The pesticides stayed inside their bodies. Then larger animals that ate the smaller animals also got sick. When humans ate those plants and animals, they got sick, too.

Rachel did a lot of research. She double-checked her facts. Her book was called *Silent Spring*. The title told people that our Earth would be silent and sad if we kept using pesticides. Rachel's hard work paid off. Soon laws were passed to limit the use of pesticides. Rachel showed the world why it is so important to take care of our planet.

NOTES

USE A DIAGRAM

Use the diagram below and the passage about Rachel Carson to answer the questions on the next page.

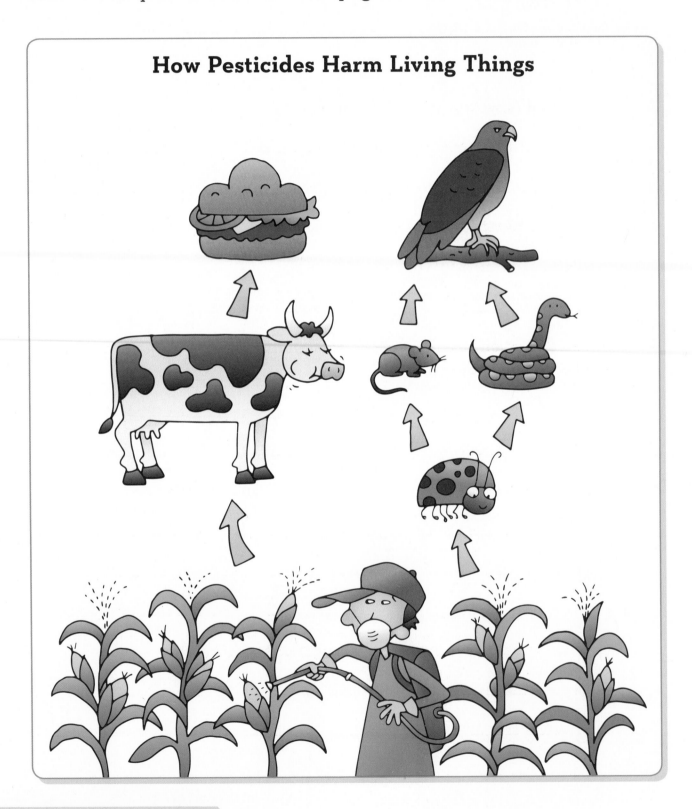

How Pesticides Harm Living Things

QUESTIONS

1. Why did Rachel leave her job at the U.S. Fish and Wildlife Service?

   _____

   _____

2. Why did Rachel write the book *Silent Spring*?

   _____

   _____

3. Do you think *Silent Spring* is a good title? Why do you think so?

   _____

   _____

4. What could happen to a mouse that eats an insect that has eaten a plant sprayed with pesticides?

   _____

   _____

5. What are three ways that birds could get sick from pesticides?

   _____

   _____

   _____

6. How could a person get sick from eating a cheeseburger?

   _____

   _____

   _____

THE APPLE MAN
Johnny Appleseed

As you read:
- Underline important words
- Circle confusing words or sentences
- Add drawings or notes to remember important facts

NOTES

_____

_____

_____

_____

_____

_____

_____

_____

_____

_____

Johnny Appleseed's real name was John Chapman. He earned his nickname by planting thousands of apple seeds across the Midwest. For this, he became a legend in his own lifetime.

Johnny was born in Massachusetts in 1774. In his teens, he learned how to grow apples. Later on, he put that knowledge to work. Settlers were going west. Johnny knew they needed fruit. So he went west, too, with a bag of apple seeds. But he didn't just scatter seeds anywhere. He cleared land and

planted apple orchards. His first orchard was in Pennsylvania. Later, he had orchards in Ohio and Indiana.

As he traveled, he visited settlers' cabins. He sold them apple seeds and seedlings. People looked forward to his visits. He brought news of other places. He told stories about his adventures.

Johnny was an unusual man. He never built a house. He liked to live in the woods. He wore shirts made out of old coffee sacks. He never wore shoes. Some say he wore a pot on his head!

Today, he is still part of our world. There are books and songs about him. There is a Johnny Appleseed Museum in Ohio. In Indiana, there is a park named for him. Johnny Appleseed's legend lives on.

NOTES

TRUE OR FALSE?

Read each statement about Johnny Appleseed. Then write **true** or **false** on the line. Use the passage on the previous page to help you.

_____ **1.** Johnny Appleseed did not wear shoes.

_____ **2.** Johnny went south with a bag of apple seeds.

_____ **3.** Johnny was born in Vermont in 1774.

_____ **4.** The settlers enjoyed Johnny's visits.

_____ **5.** Johnny's first apple orchard was in Ohio.

_____ **6.** Johnny built a log cabin for himself.

_____ **7.** Johnny sold apple seeds to settlers.

_____ **8.** Johnny Appleseed was Johnny's real name.

_____ **9.** Johnny Appleseed is remembered today.

_____ **10.** Johnny planted orchards in Pennsylvania, Ohio, and Indiana.

TRAVEL WEST IN A COVERED WAGON

Settlers who moved west had to make hard choices. They could only take the most important things on their trip. The floor of a covered wagon was about four feet wide and six to ten feet long. That's about the size of a double bed! Wagons were used for sleeping, riding, and storage.

Imagine that you are a settler traveling west with your family. Write about what you would take and what you would leave behind, and explain why.

_____

_____

_____

_____

_____

_____

_____

THE ENGINEER OF THE MODEL T
Henry Ford

As you read:

- Underline important words
- Circle confusing words or sentences
- Add drawings or notes to remember important facts

NOTES

_____

_____

_____

_____

_____

_____

_____

_____

_____

_____

Henry grew up on a farm in Dearborn, Michigan. When he was 16, he left the farm and moved to Detroit. Henry didn't want to be a farmer. He wanted to learn about engines.

Henry worked at several jobs. In 1891, he got a job at a company owned by Thomas Edison. He fixed huge steam engines. But Henry had bigger dreams. He wanted to build a gas-powered car. He spent all his free time working on this project. In 1896, Henry completed his first car. He called it the Quadricycle.

In 1903, Henry started the Ford Motor Company. Soon the first Ford car was built—the Model A. The car sold well. But Henry wanted to build a car that cost less. It had to be easy to drive and repair. It had to be light, so it could move faster. At last, in 1908, all of his ideas came together in the Model T!

Two years later, Henry came up with his assembly line. Workers assembled, or put together, each car. Each person worked on only one part. The car moved on a conveyor belt as workers added the next part. The assembly line produced cars faster, and that made the cars cheaper to buy. Henry built Model Ts this way for 19 years. He sold over 15 million of them! He became the most successful carmaker in the world.

WRITE A CAPTION

Write a caption for each picture below. Use information that you learned in the passage about Henry Ford.

Model T

_____

_____

_____

_____

_____

_____

Model T Assembly Line

_____

_____

_____

_____

_____

_____

USE A TABLE OF CONTENTS

This table of contents was taken from the book *Who Was Henry Ford?* Use the table of contents to answer the questions below.

Contents

1. In which chapter would you find information about Henry Ford's first car?

_____

2. In which chapter would you look to find out when Henry Ford died?

_____

3. How many pages of timelines are there?

_____

4. On what page does the chapter "The Model T" begin? On what page does it end?

_____

TAKEOFF WITH THE WRIGHT BROTHERS

Read each clue about the Wright brothers. Then find the answer on the next page and write it in the puzzle.

CLUES

ACROSS

1. The Wright brothers' first airplane was called the

_____.

2. The Wright brothers owned a _____ shop.

3. The science of developing and flying airplanes is

called _____.

4. The older Wright brother was _____.

DOWN

5. The first successful airplane flight was in

_____, North Carolina.

6. A person who flies an airplane is a _____.

7. The younger Wright brother was _____.

8. The Wright brothers did many experiments with aircraft

without motors, which are called _____.

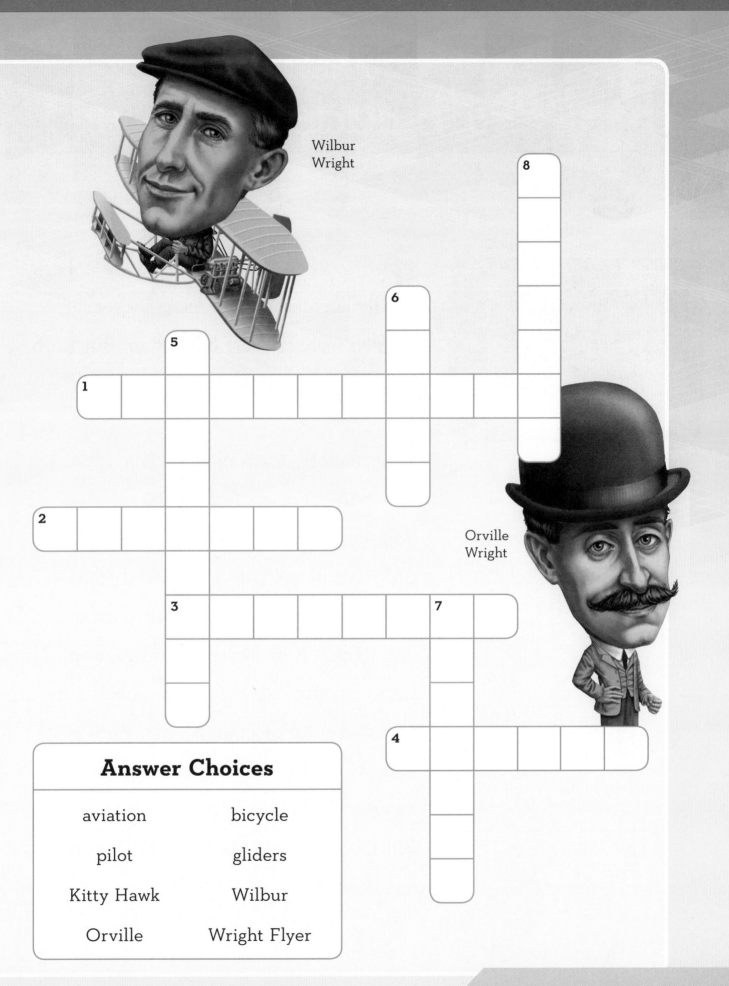

Wilbur
Wright

Orville
Wright

Answer Choices

aviation	bicycle
pilot	gliders
Kitty Hawk	Wilbur
Orville	Wright Flyer

A VOICE FOR FAIRNESS AND EQUALITY
Ruth Bader Ginsburg

As you read:

- Underline important words
- Circle confusing words or sentences
- Add drawings or notes to remember important facts

NOTES

_____

_____

_____

_____

_____

_____

_____

_____

_____

In the 1950s, when Ruth was in college, she decided to become a lawyer. Few women were lawyers back then. But Ruth made up her mind to go for it.

After college, Ruth married Marty Ginsburg. In their family, they shared household responsibilities, and Marty did most of the cooking. They had a baby daughter, and they both went to law school. Ruth graduated at the top of her class. But she got no job offers! Law firms only hired men. At last, Ruth got a job working for a judge. Then in 1963, Rutgers University hired her to teach law. But there was one problem. She got paid less than the male professors!

She helped female professors at Rutgers file a lawsuit for equal pay. They won! In the 1970s, Ruth argued six cases before the U.S. Supreme Court. In these cases, she argued for equal rights for women and men. In 1980, President Jimmy Carter made Ruth a judge. Then in 1993, President Bill Clinton chose her to be a justice on the Supreme Court! Ruth served until her death in 2020. She was known for standing up for fairness and equality. For that she is one of the most admired women in our country.

FILL IN THE CHART

In the first section, write what you knew about Ruth Bader Ginsburg before you read the passage. In the second section, write the things that you learned from the passage. In the third section, write about the things you would still like to learn.

Ruth Bader Ginsburg

What I Already Knew

_____

_____

_____

What I Learned From the Passage

_____

_____

_____

What I Would Like to Learn

_____

_____

_____

THE SUPREME COURT

Look at the photo of the Supreme Court justices from September 2020 and read the information in the caption. Then answer the questions below.

Front row, left to right:
Stephen G. Breyer, Clarence Thomas, John G. Roberts Jr. (Chief Justice), Ruth Bader Ginsburg, Samuel A. Alito Jr.

Back row, left to right:
Neil M. Gorsuch, Sonia Sotomayor, Elena Kagan, Brett M. Kavanaugh

1. The Chief Justice of the Supreme Court organizes the court's schedule. Who is the Chief Justice?

_____

2. How many Supreme Court justices are there? How many are women? How many are men?

_____

_____

3. The Supreme Court justices are appointed for life. Do you think this is a good idea? Write your opinion. Be sure to give reasons to support your opinion.

_____

_____

_____

THE PLANT DOCTOR
George Washington Carver

2015

As you read:

- Underline important words
- Circle confusing words or sentences
- Add drawings or notes to remember important facts

NOTES

_____

_____

_____

_____

_____

_____

_____

_____

_____

_____

George was born an enslaved person on a farm in Missouri one year before slavery ended. George loved taking care of the plants on the farm. He could make any plant grow! He became known as "the plant doctor."

George wanted to learn more about plants. But the school in his town did not allow Black people. So when he was 11, George left the farm. He went to school in another town. Over the next few years, he continued his education.

His goal was to go to college. And he did! When he graduated, George became a teacher.

Later on, George was invited to teach at the Tuskegee Institute. While there, he developed over 300 products made from peanuts. For example, glue, dyes, plastics, and soaps. He also came up with the idea of rotating crops. That was growing a crop like cotton one season, but growing a different crop the next. Why? Cotton takes many nutrients out of the soil. George suggested planting crops like sweet potatoes and peanuts that restored the soil. His ideas helped farmers a lot! He was known as one of the most helpful scientists in the world. He found practical ways for science to make people's lives better.

NOTES

ALL KINDS OF QUESTIONS

Use the passage on the previous page to answer these five questions about George Washington Carver.

1. **Where?** Where was George born?

_____

_____

2. **Why?** Why did George leave home?

_____

_____

_____

3. **What?** What can be made from peanuts?

_____

_____

4. **Who?** Who did George help?

_____

_____

5. **How?** How does crop rotation work?

_____

_____

_____

PARTS OF A PLANT

Read about the different parts of a plant. Then label the parts on the diagram below.

Part of a Plant	Definition
roots	the part that takes in water and nutrients from the soil
stem	the part that carries water and nutrients from the roots to the rest of the plant
leaves	the part that uses sunlight and air to make food for the plant
flower	the part that makes seeds, so that new plants can grow

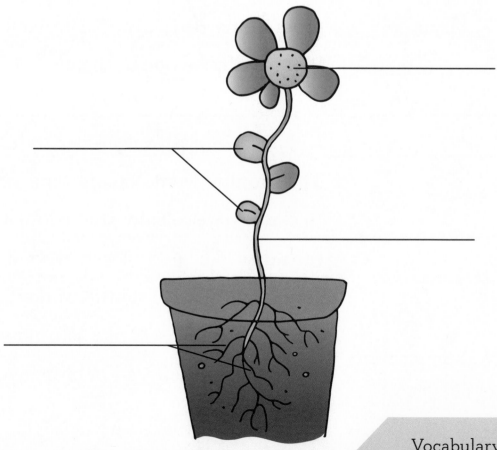

READY FOR A CHALLENGE
Sally Ride

NOTES

_____

_____

_____

_____

_____

_____

_____

_____

In 1977, Sally was a student at Stanford University. She would soon graduate. She hoped to be a scientist and teacher. One day, she was looking at job ads in the school newspaper. She saw that the U.S. space program needed astronauts. Sally applied for the job. So did more than 8,000 others! But the space program needed only 35 astronauts. Would Sally be one of them? Yes!

In July 1978, Sally began her training. The training would take several years. In the first year, Sally studied for hours each day. She had to learn every detail about how a space shuttle worked. She also studied subjects like astronomy. She had to know the location of many stars.

NOTES

Sally had to pass a lot of physical tests. She had to parachute out of planes and scuba dive in icy water. She spent time in a simulator, a model of the space shuttle. It stayed on the ground. But it vibrated and turned her upside down. It played loud noises, too. It showed her what being in space would be like. Five years went by. Sally waited for her turn to go to space. At last, in April 1982, she got the news. She was chosen to be part of the *Challenger* crew. She would be the first American woman in space!

SALLY RIDE'S TRAINING

Write six details that you learned from the passage about Sally Ride that support the main idea.

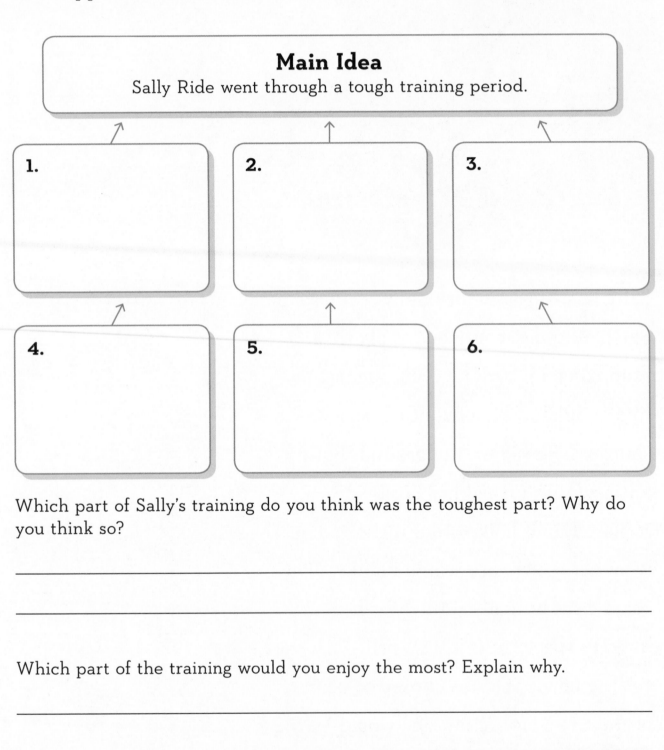

Main Idea
Sally Ride went through a tough training period.

1.

2.

3.

4.

5.

6.

Which part of Sally's training do you think was the toughest part? Why do you think so?

_____

_____

Which part of the training would you enjoy the most? Explain why.

_____

_____

INTERVIEW QUESTIONS

If you could interview Sally Ride, what questions would you want to ask her? Write your questions below.

1. **Who** _____
   _____ ?

2. **What** _____
   _____ ?

3. **Where** _____
   _____ ?

4. **When** _____
   _____ ?

5. **Why** _____
   _____ ?

6. **How** _____
   _____ ?

JOURNEY ACROSS THE NORTHWEST

In 1805, a Native American woman named Sacagawea helped guide the Lewis and Clark expedition. She was only 16 years old. She carried her baby on her back, too! When people on the expedition were hungry, she found food. When they met other Native Americans, she was their translator. Thanks to her, the expedition was a success. It helped the United States settle a huge region in the Northwest. To honor her, mountains and lakes have been named after her. Can you help Sacagawea guide the expedition to the Pacific Ocean?

PACIFIC OCEAN

AMERICAN NORTHWEST

START

WEATHER WORDS

Unscramble the words that are related to weather. Use the clues to help you. One letter in each word will go inside a box.

1. O D L U C [ ] __ __ __ __

Clue: a white or gray mass in the sky, made up of tiny drops of water

2. Z A L R D B I Z __ [ ] __ __ __ __ __ __

Clue: a snowstorm with winds of 35 miles per hour or more

3. T G I H N G N L I __ [ ] __ __ __ __ __ __ __

Clue: a flash of light when electricity moves between clouds

4. U T N U A M __ __ __ __ [ ] __

Clue: another name for the season of fall

5. B I R N W A O __ [ ] __ __ __ __ __

Clue: an arch of colored light that is composed of seven colors

6. O T N O A D R [ ] __ __ __ __ __ __

Clue: a storm with wind that spins in circles

7. R T N E H D U __ __ __ __ __ [ ] __

Clue: the noise that often follows a flash of lightning

Now write the letter from each box from top to bottom in the boxes below. A pattern of weather that is measured over time is:

[ ] [ ] [ ] [ ] [ ] [ ] [ ]

A BRAVE LEADER
Ernest Shackleton

As you read:

- Underline important words
- Circle confusing words or sentences
- Add drawings or notes to remember important facts

NOTES

In 1914, the British explorer Ernest Shackleton led a voyage to the South Pole. It was his third trip. But he hadn't reached the South Pole the other two times. Another explorer got there first. So Ernest set a new goal for this trip. He would walk across Antarctica.

Ernest named his ship *Endurance*, which means "the ability to withstand hardships." What a fitting name! When he and his team reached Antarctica, the sea was full of ice. Their ship couldn't move. Then, sharp pieces of ice cut into the ship. So

Ernest ordered his men to leave with lifeboats and supplies. The ship sank, and the men had to camp out on the ice. When the ice melted, they set off in their lifeboats. After a week at sea, they reached Elephant Island. But Ernest knew they couldn't survive there. So he made a plan. He and five men would take a lifeboat and row 800 miles to South Georgia Island! There was a whaling station there. They would get help and come back.

The six men set off in rough waters. It took 16 days to reach South Georgia Island. Then it was a 17-mile hike to the whaling station. Three men were too ill to walk. So Ernest and two others hiked for 36 hours. And they made it! Ernest never walked across Antarctica. But all of his men were rescued. Because of his brave leadership, his crew survived.

NOTES

USE A MAP

Use the map below and the passage about Ernest Shackleton to answer the questions on the next page.

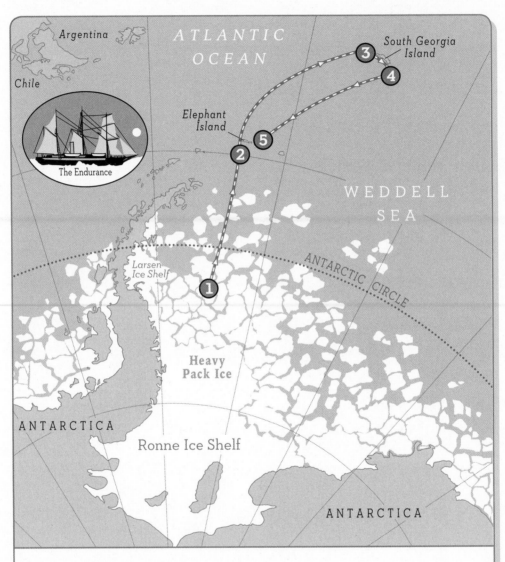

Argentina

ATLANTIC OCEAN

South Georgia Island

Chile

The Endurance

Elephant Island

WEDDELL SEA

Larsen Ice Shelf

ANTARCTIC CIRCLE

ANTARCTICA

Heavy Pack Ice

Ronne Ice Shelf

ANTARCTICA

1. *Endurance* sinks

2. Trip to Elephant Island

3. Trip to South Georgia Island

4. Walk across South Georgia Island

5. Return to Elephant Island for other men

QUESTIONS

1. What was Ernest's goal for his trip? Did he reach his goal?

   _____

   _____

2. What was the first problem that Ernest and his crew faced?

   _____

3. Why did the *Endurance* sink?

   _____

4. After the ice melted, where did Ernest and his crew go? How did they get there?

   _____

   _____

   _____

5. Who went to South Georgia Island? Why was it a difficult trip?

   _____

   _____

   _____

6. What happened to the men who were on Elephant Island?

   _____

7. What is your opinion of Ernest Shackleton?

   _____

   _____

AN IMPRESSIVE FIRST LADY
Michelle Obama

As you read:

- Underline important words
- Circle confusing words or sentences
- Add drawings or notes to remember important facts

NOTES

_____

_____

_____

_____

_____

_____

_____

_____

_____

Even before she was First Lady, Michelle had achieved a lot in her life. She went to Princeton University. Then she went to Harvard Law School. She became a lawyer. She worked for the University of Chicago. Michelle was impressive before she moved into the White House!

As First Lady, Michelle had to be a hostess. She was in charge of formal dinners when heads of countries visited. She also traveled to foreign countries to represent the U.S. But Michelle wanted to make a difference, too. So she began a program to help kids stay healthy. First, she planted a vegetable garden at the White House. She invited kids from a

local school to help. The White House chefs used the vegetables in meals for Michelle's family. She hoped that all kids would eat healthy foods. She also started a program called "Let's Move." Getting exercise was important, too. She suggested that schools stay open in the evening. Why? So families could play basketball! She encouraged towns to create bike lanes and walking paths.

Michelle was First Lady from 2009 to 2017. But during that time, she was also a mom to two girls. It couldn't have been easy to juggle all the things on her plate. But Michelle made it look easy.

MANY ACHIEVEMENTS

In the first column, write about Michelle Obama's achievements before she became First Lady. In the second column, write about her achievements as First Lady.

Michelle Obama's Achievements	
Before She Was First Lady	**As First Lady**

Which of Michelle Obama's achievements impressed you the most? Explain why.

_____

_____

_____

USE A TABLE OF CONTENTS

This table of contents was taken from the book *Who Is Michelle Obama?* Use the table of contents to answer the questions below.

Contents

1. In which chapter would you find information about how Michelle met

Barack Obama? _____

2. On what page does the chapter "A New Family" begin? On what page

does it end? _____

3. In which chapter would you find information about Michelle's role as

First Lady? _____

THE MAN WHO DISCOVERED GRAVITY
Isaac Newton

As you read:

- Underline important words
- Circle confusing words or sentences
- Add drawings or notes to remember important facts

NOTES

Isaac Newton was born in Lincolnshire, England, in 1642. At age 18, he went off to college. Few people went to college back then. But Isaac had a brilliant mind.

In the famous story about him, Isaac saw an apple fall from a tree. It made him wonder what pulled the apple toward Earth. He figured out that the force that made an apple fall to Earth was the same force that made planets orbit, or move around, the sun. Isaac gave it the name we still use today—*gravity*. He also built a more powerful telescope. He used a mirror in his telescope. That made the image much clearer.

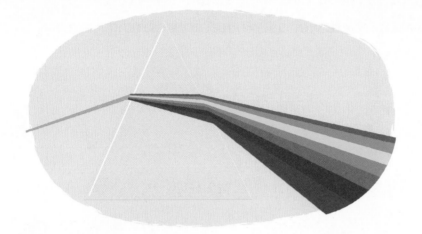

NOTES

Isaac did experiments with light, too. He used a thick triangle of glass called a *prism*. When he shone light on it, he saw the colors of the rainbow. What did he learn from his experiments? Light in its basic form was not pure white. Instead, white light was made up of seven different colors put together. The colors were red, orange, yellow, green, blue, indigo, and violet.

Isaac Newton died in 1727. He is known as one of the greatest scientists who ever lived. His ideas helped people understand how the universe works.

THREE IMPORTANT DISCOVERIES

The passage you just read describes three of Isaac Newton's important discoveries. In your own words, write something you learned about each discovery.

gravity

_____

_____

telescope

_____

_____

light

_____

_____

What would Isaac Newton think about our explorations in space today?

_____

_____

CENTER OF GRAVITY EXPERIMENT

An object's center of gravity is the spot where the weight is equal on each side.

Try this experiment:

You will need: a 12-inch ruler and a piece of clay.

1. Balance a ruler on your finger. Move the ruler left or right to find the place where it is balanced. That is its center of gravity. A ruler's center of gravity is in the middle of the ruler.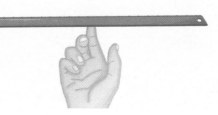

2. Put a piece of clay about one inch from the end of the ruler.

3. Now find the new center of gravity.

4. Draw a picture that shows where the center of gravity is when there is a piece of clay on the ruler. Then write a sentence that describes your picture.

WHAT DO YOU KNOW ABOUT CLARA BARTON?

Read each clue about Clara Barton. Then find the answer on the next page and write it in the puzzle.

CLUES

ACROSS

1. Clara Barton was born in _____ in 1821.

2. Clara's first job was as a _____ .

3. During the Civil War, Clara nursed wounded

_____ back to health.

DOWN

4. In 1852, Clara established the first free public school in

_____ .

5. Clara became the most famous _____ in

American history.

6. Clara was the founder and first president of

the American _____ .

7. Clara was known as the

"_____ of the battlefield."

8. Clara also fought for women's

_____ , which is the right to vote.

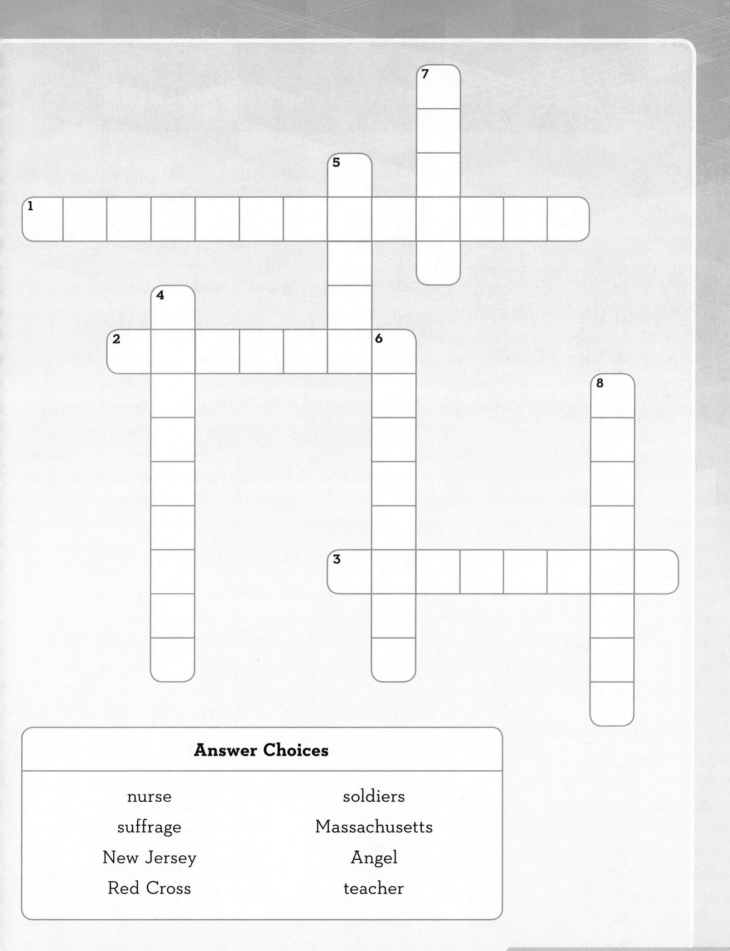

Answer Choices

nurse	soldiers
suffrage	Massachusetts
New Jersey	Angel
Red Cross	teacher

UNDERWATER EXPLORER
Jacques Cousteau

As you read:

- Underline important words
- Circle confusing words or sentences
- Add drawings or notes to remember important facts

NOTES

_____

_____

_____

_____

_____

_____

_____

_____

_____

In 1936, when Jacques was a young man, he had a car accident. His arm was badly injured. To help his arm heal, he began swimming in the sea. One day, a friend loaned him a pair of goggles. It changed his life! Jacques was amazed by the world he saw beneath the waves.

Soon he began taking photos of ocean life. So he wanted to find a way to stay underwater for a long time. Jacques worked with an engineer and invented the Aqua-Lung. The Aqua-Lung was a tank that supplied air. A swimmer could stay underwater for hours.

In 1950, Jacques bought a ship named the *Calypso*. Jacques used it to explore the world's oceans. He discovered sea life that had never been seen before and filmed it. In 1953, his first book was published: *The Silent World.* Then he made an underwater movie with the same title. His movie won many awards. Later on, Jacques became a TV star! His show was called *The Undersea World of Jacques Cousteau.*

Jacques enjoyed teaching people about the wonders of ocean life. But he also worked hard to protect the world's oceans. He wanted future generations to enjoy the beauty of the sea.

FILL IN THE CHART

Use the information that you learned about Jacques Cousteau to write facts in the four boxes of the chart below.

Inventor	Explorer
Author	**Moviemaker and TV Star**

PROTECT OUR EARTH

Think about our Earth and something on it that you would like to take care of. Describe why it is important to you and how you would protect it. Then draw a picture that shows what you would do.

_____

_____

_____

_____

_____

_____

HIGH HOPES AND DREAMS
Sonia Sotomayor

As you read:
- Underline important words
- Circle confusing words or sentences
- Add drawings or notes to remember important facts

NOTES

_____

_____

_____

_____

_____

_____

_____

_____

_____

_____

When Sonia was growing up, she watched a TV show called *Perry Mason*. It was about a clever lawyer who defended people. Sonia thought maybe she could be a lawyer like Perry Mason! She knew she'd have to study hard and get good grades. So that is what she did.

All through her school years, Sonia worked hard. During high school, she also had a part-time job. Her family was poor, and she had to help out. Sonia was pleased when she got a full scholarship

to Princeton University. That meant she didn't have to pay for school. In 1976, she graduated with honors. Then she went on to Yale Law School.

When Sonia graduated from law school, her dream came true! She became a lawyer in New York City. In fact, she was a very successful lawyer for many years. Then Sonia had a new dream. She wanted to become a judge. And of course, she did! Sonia also taught classes at six different law schools. She gave speeches all over the country, too. Life was good. Then in 2009, it got even better! She received a call from the White House. President Obama told her he would name her to be a justice on the Supreme Court. On August 8, 2009, Sonia took the oath to be a justice on the highest court in the land.

NOTES

TRUE OR FALSE?

Read each statement about Sonia Sotomayor. Write **true** or **false** on the line. Then rewrite the false statements on the lines below to make them true.

_____ **1.** When Sonia was growing up, she wanted to be a judge.

_____ **2.** Sonia got good grades without studying very much.

_____ **3.** Sonia received a scholarship to attend Princeton University.

_____ **4.** Sonia became a very successful lawyer.

_____ **5.** President Bush named Sonia to be a justice on the Supreme Court.

_____ **6.** Sonia became a Supreme Court justice in 2009.

_____

_____

_____

_____

_____

_____

_____

CAREER PATHS

When Sonia Sotomayor was a young girl, she started thinking about what she might want to be when she grew up. Now it's your turn! Write about a career that you think would be a good fit for you. Explain why you think that job would be interesting. Describe the education or training you would need to do that job. Then draw a picture that shows you at work.

_____

_____

_____

_____

_____

WORDS WERE HIS WEAPON
Frederick Douglass

As you read:

- Underline important words
- Circle confusing words or sentences
- Add drawings or notes to remember important facts

NOTES

_____

_____

_____

_____

_____

_____

_____

_____

_____

Frederick Douglass was born in 1818 in Maryland. He was born an enslaved person. Most enslaved people didn't learn how to read. It was against the law! But he taught himself to read and write. In 1838, Frederick decided to escape to the North. He had tried to escape before and had failed. But he wasn't a person who gave up.

This time, Frederick arrived safely in New York. Then he moved to New Bedford, Massachusetts. In 1841, he attended a meeting of the American Anti-Slavery Society. He was asked to speak about his experiences as an enslaved person. What a powerful speaker he was! The society hired him to give speeches all around the country. In 1845, he wrote a book about his experiences. It became an instant best seller.

Now Frederick was in danger. He could be captured by his former owners. So he went to England, where an amazing thing happened. His English friends raised money to buy his freedom! Frederick returned to America. He began to publish an antislavery newspaper. He called it *The North Star*. It was named after the star that guided enslaved people to their freedom after they had run away. Frederick also fought for voting rights for Black people and for women. Using words as his weapon, he spent his life fighting for equal rights for all.

SHOW WHAT YOU KNOW

Put the following events in the life of Frederick Douglass in the correct order by numbering them from 1 to 10.

☐ Frederick attended a meeting of the American Anti-Slavery Society.

☐ Frederick went to England for a while.

☐ Frederick was born an enslaved person in Maryland.

☐ Frederick's book was an instant best seller.

☐ Frederick published an antislavery newspaper called *The North Star.*

☐ Frederick arrived in New York.

☐ Frederick was hired to give speeches around the country.

☐ Frederick moved to New Bedford, Massachusetts.

☐ Frederick decided to escape to the North.

☐ Frederick returned to America after he was freed.

WHAT WOULD FREDERICK DOUGLASS THINK?

If Frederick Douglass could visit our world today, what would he think of it? What are some things he would be happy about? What are some things he would still want to change?

_____

_____

_____

_____

_____

_____

_____

_____

_____

_____

_____

FACTS ABOUT MARTIN LUTHER KING JR.

Read some facts about Martin Luther King Jr.'s life.
Then find the **bold-faced** words in the word search.

G	M	R	U	O	D	H	C	N	A	L	R
C	I	V	I	L	R	I	G	H	T	S	D
Y	N	V	N	Q	E	G	B	S	L	N	E
Z	I	L	J	B	A	U	Z	K	A	M	Q
E	S	K	V	D	M	C	S	M	N	V	U
Q	T	U	A	K	J	D	F	G	T	C	A
P	E	A	C	E	F	U	L	R	A	X	L
W	R	G	R	M	T	J	T	D	Z	V	I
S	X	L	A	U	B	O	Y	C	O	T	T
R	D	N	E	K	D	A	C	J	L	R	Y

Martin Luther King Jr. was born in **Atlanta**, Georgia, in 1929.

When Martin graduated from college, he became a **minister**.

Later on, he became a **civil rights** leader.

Martin believed in **peaceful**, or nonviolent, protest.

He led the bus **boycott** in Montgomery, Alabama.

Martin gave his famous "I Have a **Dream**" speech in 1963.

Today, people remember all that he did to fight for **equality**.

WHAT'S THE QUESTION?

Write the question that goes with each answer. Use the pictures of famous people to help you. The first one has been done for you.

1. **Question:** Who was George Washington?

   Answer: He was a brave general and our country's first president.

2. **Question:** _____

   Answer: She was the First Lady for 12 years and helped start the United Nations.

3. **Question:** _____

   Answer: He was the first secretary of the treasury, and his picture is on the ten-dollar bill.

4. **Question:** _____

   Answer: She fought for a woman's right to vote but did not live to see it happen.

5. **Question:** _____

   Answer: He was our 16th president and is known as one of our greatest presidents ever.

6. **Question:** _____

   Answer: She was the first woman to fly solo across the Atlantic Ocean.

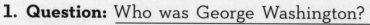

7. **Question:** _____

   Answer: He spoke out against slavery and spent his life fighting for equal rights.

THE MOST FAMOUS WOMAN IN SCIENCE
Marie Curie

As you read:
- Underline important words
- Circle confusing words or sentences
- Add drawings or notes to remember important facts

NOTES

_____

_____

_____

_____

_____

_____

_____

_____

_____

Marie was born in Poland in 1867. She was a smart and curious girl. Marie wanted to be a scientist. But the colleges in Poland didn't allow women! So she moved to France to attend the Sorbonne. It was a famous university that accepted women. Marie worked hard. She graduated as the top student in her class! Later on, she met a French scientist named Pierre Curie. They got married in 1895.

The Curies set up a lab together. Marie began to study a type of energy called *radioactive rays*. These rays came from certain metals. Through her research, she discovered two new metals. She named them *polonium* and *radium*.

Radium was very powerful. It glowed in the dark. Later on, it was used to treat cancer. But Marie didn't realize that handling it was harmful. Radium could damage your skin and bones.

In 1903, Marie and Pierre won a Nobel Prize. It is one of the highest honors for a scientist. The Curies became very famous. Then in 1911, Marie won a second Nobel Prize! This time, she alone was the winner. Only three other people have ever won the Nobel Prize twice. Marie died in 1934. The radium had weakened her body. Today, she remains the most famous woman in science.

ALL KINDS OF QUESTIONS

Use the passage on the previous page to answer these five questions about Marie Curie.

1. **Where?** Where was Marie born?

_____

2. **Why?** Why did Marie move to France?

_____

_____

_____

3. **Who?** Who won the Nobel Prize with Marie in 1903?

_____

_____

_____

4. **What?** What metals did Marie discover?

_____

_____

_____

5. **When?** When did Marie win her second Nobel Prize?

_____

_____

_____

COMPARE AND CONTRAST

How were Marie Curie and Sally Ride alike? How were they different? Write about it on the lines below. You may want to reread the passage about Sally Ride on pages 42-43.

Alike

_____

_____

_____

_____

_____

_____

Different

_____

_____

_____

_____

_____

A GREAT INVENTOR AND TEACHER
Alexander Graham Bell

As you read:
- Underline important words
- Circle confusing words or sentences
- Add drawings or notes to remember important facts

NOTES

Alexander Graham Bell is best known for inventing the telephone. But all his life, he also worked to help the deaf. His mother was nearly deaf, and they were very close. So he was always interested in working with sound and speech.

Alexander was teaching at the Boston School for the Deaf in 1871. But he had time to work on his inventions, too. He hired a man named Thomas Watson as his assistant. Alexander wanted to invent a machine that could transmit voices through wire. Soon he had a rough model of his telephone. In 1876, he received a patent for it. A patent is proof from the government that an inventor's idea belongs to him or her.

Alexander worked in his laboratory to improve the telephone. In 1877, the Bell Telephone Company was formed. Orders were pouring in. People realized that this new device was life-changing. Alexander became rich. But he kept on inventing. He made a machine to test people's hearing. It was called an *audiometer*. He worked with another man to invent a *metal detector*. This machine clicked loudly when it got close to metal. Alexander died in 1922. On the day he was buried, all telephone service in the U.S. stopped for one minute. It was a perfect way to honor this great inventor and teacher.

TARGET SCIENCE VOCABULARY

Choose the word or term from the word bank that completes each sentence.

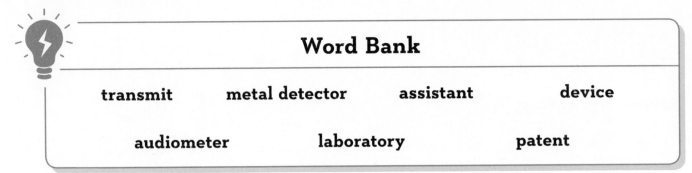

Word Bank

transmit	**metal detector**	**assistant**	**device**
audiometer	**laboratory**		**patent**

1. A room where scientists or inventors work is called a

   _____ .

2. An _____ is a person who helps, or assists, with a

   task or job.

3. When you _____ voices or signals through a wire,

   you send them out.

4. A _____ is proof from the government that an

   inventor's idea belongs to him or her.

5. Something that is invented for a particular use or purpose is called

   a _____ .

6. A _____ is a machine that can find,

   or detect, the presence of metal.

7. A machine that is used to measure how well a person

   can hear is an _____ .

ALEXANDER GRAHAM BELL
SUMMARY FRAME

Before I read the passage, I knew _____ about

Alexander Graham Bell.

One important thing I learned was _____

_____

_____ .

I also found out that _____

_____ .

Another fact I discovered was _____

_____ .

One fact that surprised me was _____

_____ .

Some questions that I have about Alexander Graham Bell are:

_____

_____

_____

_____

_____

A GENERAL AND A PRESIDENT
Ulysses S. Grant

As you read:

- Underline important words
- Circle confusing words or sentences
- Add drawings or notes to remember important facts

NOTES

_____

_____

_____

_____

_____

_____

_____

_____

When the Civil War ended in 1865, Ulysses S. Grant was a hero. He was the most popular man in the country—more popular than President Abraham Lincoln! Why was he so admired? He was a brave general. He won many battles. His men respected him, too. In 1864, President Lincoln had put him in charge of the entire Union army. He was named a lieutenant general. The only other soldier ever given that title at this time was George Washington!

In 1868, Ulysses ran for president and won. But as president, he was both a success and a failure. He supported voting rights for Black people. He helped keep the peace after the war. But he also made mistakes. He wasn't a good judge of character. It turned out that many people who worked for him were dishonest. Some stole millions of dollars in tax money. Even so, Ulysses was reelected and served two terms.

In 1885, he became very ill. He knew he had only months to live. So he began to write his memoirs, the story of his life. A few days after he finished his book, he died. At his funeral, four generals from the Civil War helped carry his casket. Two were from the North, and two were from the South.

Personal Memoirs of U. S. Grant

USE A TIMELINE

Use the timeline below and the passage about Ulysses S. Grant to answer the questions on the next page.

Timeline of Ulysses S. Grant's Life

1822 Is born Hiram Ulysses Grant on April 27 in Point Pleasant, Ohio

1839 Attends West Point Military Academy
Adopts the name Ulysses S. Grant

1843 Graduates West Point and becomes an officer in the army

1848 Marries Julia Dent

1850 The Grants' first child, Frederick Dent Grant, is born

1854 Quits the army and returns to his family

1860 South Carolina secedes from the Union

1861 Civil War begins
Returns to the army as a volunteer to fight in the Civil War

1864 President Lincoln appoints Grant lieutenant general

1865 General Robert E. Lee surrenders, ending the Civil War

1869 Ulysses S. Grant is sworn in as president of the
United States on March 4

1872 Reelected president

1885 Writes his memoirs
Dies at 63 years old

QUESTIONS

1. When did Ulysses S. Grant graduate from West Point Military Academy?

_____

2. Did President Lincoln have confidence in Ulysses S. Grant?
Give two facts to support your answer.

_____

_____

_____

3. When did the Civil War begin? When did it end?

_____

_____

4. Name one good thing and one bad thing about his presidency.

_____

_____

_____

5. When did Ulysses write his memoirs? How old was he when he died?

_____

_____

6. What do you think was Ulysses S. Grant's most important
accomplishment? Explain why.

_____

_____

LAUGH OUT LOUD!

Write the answer to each joke. Use the answer choices in the box on the next page.

What would you get if you crossed the first U.S. president with an animated character?

_____

Why did Marie Curie listen to music?

_____

What did Johnny Appleseed say when his tree sprouted?

_____

Why was Amelia Earhart such a great pilot?

_____

Why did Paul Revere ride his horse from Boston to Lexington?

_____

What did Ernest Shackleton say when he first saw penguins in Antarctica?

_____

Where did Sally Ride leave her spaceship?

_____

Why did Davy Crockett wear a crown?

_____

Why did Queen Victoria always measure things?

_____

What did Henry Ford say when he opened his first car factory?

_____

Answer Choices

At a parking *meteor*!

"I'm *wheelie* excited!"

Because the horse was too heavy to carry!

Because she loved *radio*-activity!

George Washing-*toon*!

"Look at those *brrrrrrr*-ds!"

Because he was *King* of the Wild Frontier!

Because she was a *ruler*!

Because she had a very positive *altitude*!

"*Seedling* is believing!"

LAUGH OUT LOUD!

Write the answer to each joke. Use the answer choices in the box on the next page.

What did the sheep say when he saw President Obama?
__"Hi, Baaaaa-rack!"__

Why were Betsy Ross's feet tired?
__Because of her American indepen-dance!__

When did Abraham Lincoln make meatballs?
__During the Spaghetti-sburg Address!__

Why did Michelle Obama win the marathon?
__Because she was the First Lady to cross the finish line!__

Why do cows like Neil Armstrong?
__Because he was the first man on the moooooooo-n!__

Why did Thomas Edison read so much about electricity?
__Because he liked current events!__

4

Why was Sally Ride so hungry?
__Because she forgot to eat her launch!__

Why did Orville and Wilbur Wright like to stay inside?
__Because they were in-ventors!__

Why did Amelia Earhart want to fly around the world?
__Because life at home was too plane!__

What did Ben Franklin say after discovering that lightning was electricity?
__"I am shocked!"__

Answer Choices

"I am shocked!"	Because she was the First Lady to cross the finish line!
Because he liked current events!	Because they were in-ventors!
Because life at home was too plane!	Because of her American indepen-dance!
Because she forgot to eat her launch!	Because he was the first man on the moooooooo-n!
During the Spaghetti-sburg Address!	"Hi, Baaaaa-rack!"

5

FIND THE FACTS

Use the map to answer questions 1–2. Use the passage about Paul Revere to answer questions 3–5.

1. Which city is farther from Boston—New York City or Philadelphia?
Philadelphia is farther from Boston.

2. In what direction was Paul Revere traveling when he rode to these cities?
He was traveling in a southwest direction.

3. What role did Paul play in the American Revolution?
He was a messenger who spread the news about the Revolution.

4. What secret group did Paul belong to?
He belonged to the Sons of Liberty.

5. What was the purpose of the Boston Tea Party?
The purpose was to destroy the tea, so that no taxes would be paid to the British.

8

THEN AND NOW

Paul Revere traveled by horseback to share important news. Fill in the chart to show the different ways people may have traveled and communicated in colonial times and the different ways people travel and communicate now.

Then	
Travel	**Communication**
walking	talking
horses	letters/mail
horses and wagons	newspapers
boats and ships	books

Now	
Travel	**Communication**
walking, bicycles, cars, trucks, trains, buses, boats and ships, airplanes, helicopters, spacecraft	talking, letters/mail, newspapers, books, telephones, mobile phones, computers, tablets, TVs, radios

Tell about some of the ways that you travel and communicate with your family and friends.
Answers will vary.

9

QUESTIONS

1. Where and when was Rosa Parks born?
Rosa Parks was born in Tuskegee, Alabama, in 1913.

2. When did Rosa receive her high school diploma? Why did it take so long?
Rosa received her high school diploma in 1934. She had to quit high school when she was younger to take care of her grandmother.

3. What role did Rosa have in the NAACP?
She became secretary of the Montgomery chapter of the NAACP.

4. Rosa's refusal to give up her seat on the bus had big effects. What were they?
Rosa was arrested. Her arrest led to a bus boycott. The boycott led to a change in the laws. There would be no more "whites only" seats on buses.

5. What honors did Rosa receive?
Rosa received the Presidential Medal of Freedom and the Congressional Medal of Honor.

6. What impressed you the most about Rosa Parks?
Answers will vary.

13

TARGET SCIENCE VOCABULARY

Choose the word from the word bank that completes each sentence.

Word Bank

kinetograph	lightbulb	sound
phonograph	invention	kinetoscope

1. Anything that can be heard can be called a __sound__.
2. A __lightbulb__ has a glass covering and produces light from an electric current.
3. A machine that records and plays back sounds is a __phonograph__.
4. People used a __kinetoscope__ to view early movies, or moving pictures.
5. When people make or design something that didn't exist before, they create a new __invention__.
6. The __kinetograph__ was a kind of camera for taking a series of moving pictures.

What does it mean to be an inventor? Define the word, and tell what traits an inventor would probably have.
Answers will vary.

16

90 Answer Key

THREE IMPORTANT INVENTIONS

The passage you just read focused on three of Thomas Edison's important inventions. In your own words, write something you learned about each invention.

phonograph

Answers will vary.

↓

long-lasting lightbulb

Answers will vary.

↓

kinetograph

Answers will vary.

Now write down some of the different ways electric lights are used (inside and outside) today.

Answers will vary.

(17)

GREAT SCIENTISTS

Read about some great scientists and their achievements. Then find the **bold-faced** words in the word search.

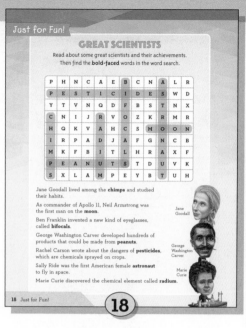

P	H	N	C	A	E	B	C	N	A	L	R
P	E	S	T	I	C	I	D	E	S	W	D
Y	T	V	N	Q	D	F	B	S	T	N	X
C	N	I	J	R	V	O	Z	K	R	M	R
H	Q	K	V	A	H	C	S	M	O	O	N
I	R	P	A	D	J	A	F	G	N	C	B
M	K	F	B	I	T	L	H	R	A	X	F
P	E	A	N	U	T	S	T	D	U	V	K
S	X	L	A	M	P	E	Y	B	T	U	H

Jane Goodall lived among the **chimps** and studied their habits.

As commander of Apollo 11, Neil Armstrong was the first man on the **moon**.

Ben Franklin invented a new kind of eyeglasses, called **bifocals**.

George Washington Carver developed hundreds of products that could be made from **peanuts**.

Rachel Carson wrote about the dangers of **pesticides**, which are chemicals sprayed on crops.

Sally Ride was the first American female **astronaut** to fly in space.

Marie Curie discovered the chemical element called **radium**.

Jane Goodall

George Washington Carver

Marie Curie

(18)

CRACK THE CODE

Crack the code to find answers to questions about famous people in history.

| A | B | C | D | E | F | G | H | I | J | K | L | M |
| 1 | 2 | 3 | 4 | 5 | 6 | 7 | 8 | 9 | 10 | 11 | 12 | 13 |

| N | O | P | Q | R | S | T | U | V | W | X | Y | Z |
| 14 | 15 | 16 | 17 | 18 | 19 | 20 | 21 | 22 | 23 | 24 | 25 | 26 |

1. Who made an 11,000-mile trip from Venice, Italy, to China and back?
M A R C O   P O L O
13 1 18 3 15   16 15 12 15

2. Who fought for a woman's right to vote?
S U S A N   B   A N T H O N Y
19 21 19 1 14   2   1 14 20 8 15 14 25

3. Who was the first Black president of South Africa?
N E L S O N   M A N D E L A
14 5 12 19 15 14   13 1 14 4 5 12 1

4. Who helped Lewis and Clark travel across the American Northwest?
S A C A G A W E A
19 1 3 1 7 1 23 5 1

5. Who signed the Declaration of Independence and was a U.S. president?
T H O M A S   J E F F E R S O N
20 8 15 13 1 19   10 5 6 6 5 18 19 15 14

(19)

QUESTIONS

1. Why did Rachel leave her job at the U.S. Fish and Wildlife Service?
She wanted to spend all her time writing about the natural world.

2. Why did Rachel write the book *Silent Spring*?
She wanted to warn people about the dangers of pesticides.

3. Do you think *Silent Spring* is a good title? Why do you think so?
Answers will vary.

4. What could happen to a mouse that eats an insect that has eaten a plant sprayed with pesticides?
That mouse could get sick or die.

5. What are three ways that birds could get sick from pesticides?
Birds could get sick from eating infected insects. They could get sick from eating infected rodents and snakes. They could also get sick from eating sprayed plants or crops.

6. How could a person get sick from eating a cheeseburger?
If the meat in the cheeseburger came from a cow that ate plants or crops sprayed with pesticides, the person who eats the cheeseburger could get sick.

(23)

TRUE OR FALSE?

Read each statement about Johnny Appleseed. Then write **true** or **false** on the line. Use the passage on the previous page to help you.

true	1. Johnny Appleseed did not wear shoes.
false	2. Johnny went south with a bag of apple seeds.
false	3. Johnny was born in Vermont in 1774.
true	4. The settlers enjoyed Johnny's visits.
false	5. Johnny's first apple orchard was in Ohio.
false	6. Johnny built a log cabin for himself.
true	7. Johnny sold apple seeds to settlers.
false	8. Johnny Appleseed was Johnny's real name.
true	9. Johnny Appleseed is remembered today.
true	10. Johnny planted orchards in Pennsylvania, Ohio, and Indiana.

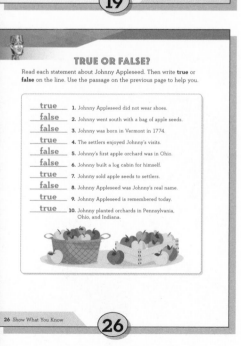

(26)

TRAVEL WEST IN A COVERED WAGON

Settlers who moved west had to make hard choices. They could only take the most important things on their trip. The floor of a covered wagon was about four feet wide and six to ten feet long. That's about the size of a double bed! Wagons were used for sleeping, riding, and storage.

Imagine that you are a settler traveling west with your family. Write about what you would take and what you would leave behind, and explain why.

Answers will vary.

(27)

WRITE A CAPTION

Write a caption for each picture below. Use information that you learned in the passage about Henry Ford.

Model T

Answers will vary.

Model T Assembly Line

Answers will vary.

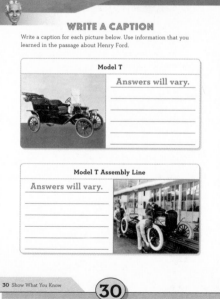

(30)

Answer Key **91**

USE A TABLE OF CONTENTS

This table of contents was taken from the book *Who Was Henry Ford?* Use the table of contents to answer the questions below.

1. In which chapter would you find information about Henry Ford's first car?
   The First Ford Car

2. In which chapter would you look to find out when Henry Ford died?
   Last Years

3. How many pages of timelines are there?
   There are two pages of timelines: pages 102 and 103.

4. On what page does the chapter "The Model T" begin? On what page does it end?
   It begins on page 47 and ends on page 67.

TAKEOFF WITH THE WRIGHT BROTHERS

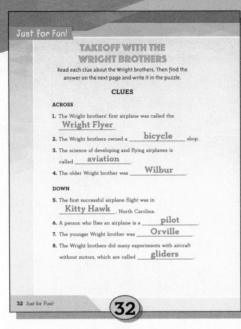

Read each clue about the Wright brothers. Then find the answer on the next page and write it in the puzzle.

CLUES

ACROSS

1. The Wright brothers' first airplane was called the **Wright Flyer**
2. The Wright brothers owned a **bicycle** shop.
3. The science of developing and flying airplanes is called **aviation**
4. The older Wright brother was **Wilbur**

DOWN

5. The first successful airplane flight was in **Kitty Hawk**, North Carolina.
6. A person who flies an airplane is a **pilot**
7. The younger Wright brother was **Orville**
8. The Wright brothers did many experiments with aircraft without motors, which are called **gliders**

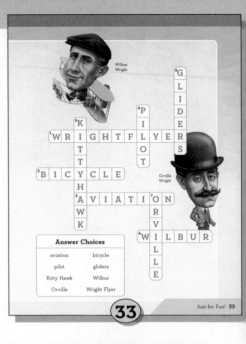

Wilbur Wright

Orville Wright

Crossword puzzle solution:
- ¹WRIGHTFLYER
- ²BICYCLE
- ³AVIATION
- ⁴WILBUR
- Down: ⁵KITTYHAWK, ⁶PILOT, ⁷ORVILLE, ⁸GLIDERS

Answer Choices

aviation	bicycle
pilot	gliders
Kitty Hawk	Wilbur
Orville	Wright Flyer

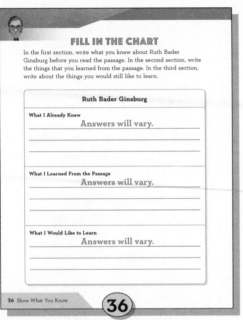

FILL IN THE CHART

In the first section, write what you knew about Ruth Bader Ginsburg before you read the passage. In the second section, write the things that you learned from the passage. In the third section, write about the things you would still like to learn.

Ruth Bader Ginsburg
What I Already Knew
Answers will vary.
What I Learned From the Passage
Answers will vary.
What I Would Like to Learn
Answers will vary.

THE SUPREME COURT

Look at the photo of the Supreme Court justices from September 2020 and read the information in the caption. Then answer the questions below.

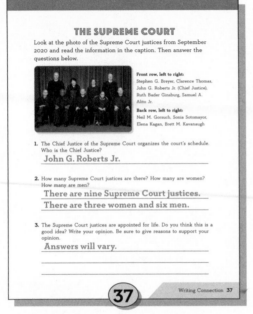

Front row, left to right:
Stephen G. Breyer, Clarence Thomas, John G. Roberts Jr. (Chief Justice), Ruth Bader Ginsburg, Samuel A. Alito Jr.

Back row, left to right:
Neil M. Gorsuch, Sonia Sotomayor, Elena Kagan, Brett M. Kavanaugh

1. The Chief Justice of the Supreme Court organizes the court's schedule. Who is the Chief Justice?
   John G. Roberts Jr.

2. How many Supreme Court justices are there? How many are women? How many are men?
   There are nine Supreme Court justices.
   There are three women and six men.

3. The Supreme Court justices are appointed for life. Do you think this is a good idea? Write your opinion. Be sure to give reasons to support your opinion.
   Answers will vary.

ALL KINDS OF QUESTIONS

Use the passage on the previous page to answer these five questions about George Washington Carver.

1. **Where?** Where was George born?
   George was born on a farm in Missouri.

2. **Why?** Why did George leave home?
   George wanted to go to school, and the school in his town didn't allow Black people.

3. **What?** What can be made from peanuts?
   Products include glue, dyes, plastics, and soaps.

4. **Who?** Who did George help?
   George helped the farmers.

5. **How?** How does crop rotation work?
   That is when a farmer grows one crop in one season, and then grows a different crop the next season.

PARTS OF A PLANT

Read about the different parts of a plant. Then label the parts on the diagram below.

Part of a Plant	Definition
roots	the part that takes in water and nutrients from the soil
stem	the part that carries water and nutrients from the roots to the rest of the plant
leaves	the part that uses sunlight and air to make food for the plant
flower	the part that makes seeds, so that new plants can grow

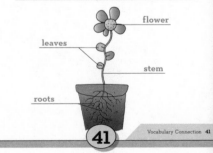

flower

leaves

stem

roots

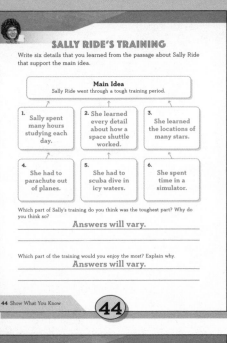

SALLY RIDE'S TRAINING

Write six details that you learned from the passage about Sally Ride that support the main idea.

Main Idea
Sally Ride went through a tough training period.

1. Sally spent many hours studying each day.
2. She learned every detail about how a space shuttle worked.
3. She learned the locations of many stars.
4. She had to parachute out of planes.
5. She had to scuba dive in icy waters.
6. She spent time in a simulator.

Which part of Sally's training do you think was the toughest part? Why do you think so?
Answers will vary.

Which part of the training would you enjoy the most? Explain why.
Answers will vary.

44

If you could interview Sally Ride, what questions would you want to ask her? Write your questions below.

1. Who **Questions will vary.**
2. What _____?
3. Where _____?
4. When _____?
5. Why _____?
6. How _____?
   _____?

45

Just for Fun!

JOURNEY ACROSS THE NORTHWEST

In 1805, a Native American woman named Sacagawea helped guide the Lewis and Clark expedition. She was only 16 years old. She carried her baby on her back, too! When people on the expedition were hungry, she found food. When they met other Native Americans, she was their translator. Thanks to her, the expedition was a success. It helped the United States settle a huge region in the Northwest. To honor her, mountains and lakes have been named after her. Can you help Sacagawea guide the expedition to the Pacific Ocean?

PACIFIC OCEAN ★

AMERICAN NORTHWEST

START

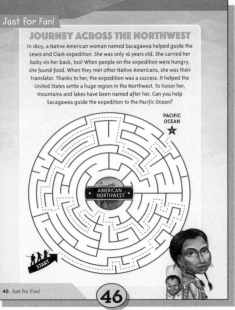

46

WEATHER WORDS

Unscramble the words that are related to weather. Use the clues to help you. One letter in each word will go inside a box.

1. ODLUC C L O U D
   Clue: a white or gray mass in the sky, made up of tiny drops of water

2. ZALRDBIZ B L I Z Z A R D
   Clue: a snowstorm with winds of 35 miles per hour or more

3. TGIHNGNLI L I G H T N I N G
   Clue: a flash of light when electricity moves between clouds

4. UTNUAM A U T U M N
   Clue: another name for the season of fall

5. BIRNWAO R A I N B O W
   Clue: an arch of colored light that is composed of seven colors

6. OTNOADR T O R N A D O
   Clue: a storm with wind that spins in circles

7. RTNEHDU T H U N D E R
   Clue: the noise that often follows a flash of lightning

Now write the letter from each box from top to bottom in the boxes below. A pattern of weather that is measured over time is:

C L I M A T E

47

QUESTIONS

1. What was Ernest's goal for his trip? Did he reach his goal?
   Ernest's goal was to walk across Antarctica, but he didn't reach his goal.

2. What was the first problem that Ernest and his crew faced?
   When they reached Antarctica, the sea was full of ice. The ship couldn't move.

3. Why did the *Endurance* sink?
   Sharp pieces of ice cut into the ship.

4. After the ice melted, where did Ernest and his crew go? How did they get there?
   They used lifeboats to get to Elephant Island.

5. Who went to South Georgia Island? Why was it a difficult trip?
   Ernest and five of his men took a lifeboat and rowed 800 miles to South Georgia Island. The sea was rough, and it took them 16 days to get there. Then it was a 17-mile hike to the whaling station.

6. What happened to the men who were on Elephant Island?
   They were rescued.

7. What is your opinion of Ernest Shackleton?
   Answers will vary.

51

MANY ACHIEVEMENTS

In the first column, write about Michelle Obama's achievements before she became First Lady. In the second column, write about her achievements as First Lady.

Michelle Obama's Achievements	
Before She Was First Lady	**As First Lady**
Examples:	Examples:
She went to Princeton University.	She was in charge of formal dinners.
She attended Harvard Law School.	She traveled to foreign countries to represent the U.S.
She was a lawyer.	She invited kids to help plant a vegetable garden at the White House.
She worked for the University of Chicago.	She started a program called "Let's Move," so kids could get more exercise.

Which of Michelle Obama's achievements impressed you the most? Explain why.
Answers will vary.

54

USE A TABLE OF CONTENTS

This table of contents was taken from the book *Who Is Michelle Obama?* Use the table of contents to answer the questions below.

1. In which chapter would you find information about how Michelle met Barack Obama? **Meeting Barack**

2. On what page does the chapter "A New Family" begin? On what page does it end? **It begins on page 50 and ends on page 59.**

3. In which chapter would you find information about Michelle's role as First Lady? **First Lady**

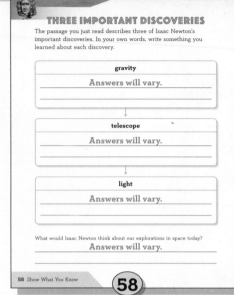

THREE IMPORTANT DISCOVERIES

The passage you just read describes three of Isaac Newton's important discoveries. In your own words, write something you learned about each discovery.

gravity
Answers will vary.

↓

telescope
Answers will vary.

↓

light
Answers will vary.

What would Isaac Newton think about our explorations in space today? **Answers will vary.**

CENTER OF GRAVITY EXPERIMENT

An object's center of gravity is the spot where the weight is equal on each side.

Try this experiment:

You will need: a 12-inch ruler and a piece of clay.

1. Balance a ruler on your finger. Move the ruler left or right to find the place where it is balanced. That is its center of gravity. A ruler's center of gravity is in the middle of the ruler.

2. Put a piece of clay about one inch from the end of the ruler.

3. Now find the new center of gravity.

4. Draw a picture that shows where the center of gravity is when there is a piece of clay on the ruler. Then write a sentence that describes your picture.

> The picture should show that the new center of gravity is closer to the piece of clay.

The center of gravity is now closer to the piece of clay.

Just for Fun!

WHAT DO YOU KNOW ABOUT CLARA BARTON?

Read each clue about Clara Barton. Then find the answer on the next page and write it in the puzzle.

CLUES

ACROSS

1. Clara Barton was born in **Massachusetts** in 1821.
2. Clara's first job was as a **teacher**.
3. During the Civil War, Clara nursed wounded **soldiers** back to health.

DOWN

4. In 1852, Clara established the first free public school in **New Jersey**.
5. Clara became the most famous **nurse** in American history.
6. Clara was the founder and first president of the American **Red Cross**.
7. Clara was known as the "**Angel** of the battlefield."
8. Clara also fought for women's **suffrage**, which is the right to vote.

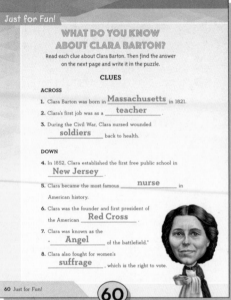

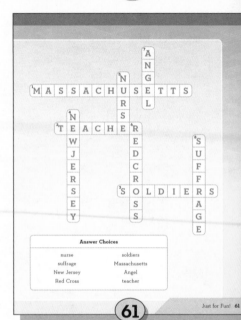

Crossword puzzle:
- ²ANGEL
- ⁵NURSE
- ¹MASSACHUSETTS
- ⁴NEW JERSEY
- ²TEACHER
- ⁶RED CROSS
- ⁸SUFFRAGE
- ³SOLDIERS

Answer Choices

nurse	soldiers
suffrage	Massachusetts
New Jersey	Angel
Red Cross	teacher

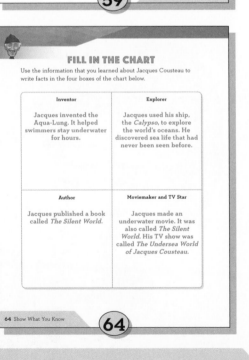

FILL IN THE CHART

Use the information that you learned about Jacques Cousteau to write facts in the four boxes of the chart below.

Inventor	Explorer
Jacques invented the Aqua-Lung. It helped swimmers stay underwater for hours.	Jacques used his ship, the *Calypso*, to explore the world's oceans. He discovered sea life that had never been seen before.
Author	**Moviemaker and TV Star**
Jacques published a book called *The Silent World*.	Jacques made an underwater movie. It was also called *The Silent World*. His TV show was called *The Undersea World of Jacques Cousteau*.

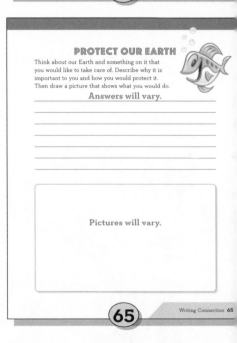

PROTECT OUR EARTH

Think about our Earth and something on it that you would like to take care of. Describe why it is important to you and how you would protect it. Then draw a picture that shows what you would do.

Answers will vary.

Pictures will vary.

TRUE OR FALSE?

Read each statement about Sonia Sotomayor. Write **true** or **false** on the line. Then rewrite the false statements on the lines below to make them true.

false   1. When Sonia was growing up, she wanted to be a judge.

false   2. Sonia got good grades without studying very much.

true   3. Sonia received a scholarship to attend Princeton University.

true   4. Sonia became a very successful lawyer.

false   5. President Bush named Sonia to be a justice on the Supreme Court.

true   6. Sonia became a Supreme Court justice in 2009.

1. When Sonia was growing up, she wanted to be a lawyer.

2. Sonia studied hard in order to get good grades.

5. President Obama named Sonia to be a justice on the Supreme Court.

68 Show What You Know

CAREER PATHS

When Sonia Sotomayor was a young girl, she started thinking about what she might want to be when she grew up. Now it's your turn! Write about a career that you think would be a good fit for you. Explain why you think that job would be interesting. Describe the education or training you would need to do that job. Then draw a picture that shows you at work.

Answers will vary.

Pictures will vary.

Writing Connection 69

SHOW WHAT YOU KNOW

Put the following events in the life of Frederick Douglass in the correct order by numbering them from 1 to 10.

5   Frederick attended a meeting of the American Anti-Slavery Society.

8   Frederick went to England for a while.

1   Frederick was born an enslaved person in Maryland.

7   Frederick's book was an instant best seller.

10   Frederick published an antislavery newspaper called *The North Star*.

3   Frederick arrived in New York.

6   Frederick was hired to give speeches around the country.

4   Frederick moved to New Bedford, Massachusetts.

2   Frederick decided to escape to the North.

9   Frederick returned to America after he was freed.

72 Show What You Know

WHAT WOULD FREDERICK DOUGLASS THINK?

If Frederick Douglass could visit our world today, what would he think of it? What are some things he would be happy about? What are some things he would still want to change?

Answers will vary.

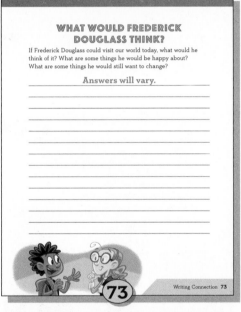

Writing Connection 73

Just for Fun!

FACTS ABOUT MARTIN LUTHER KING JR.

Read some facts about Martin Luther King Jr.'s life. Then find the **bold-faced** words in the word search.

G	M	R	U	O	D	H	C	N	A	L	R
C	I	V	I	L	R	I	G	H	T	S	D
Y	N	V	N	Q	E	G	B	S	L	N	E
Z	I	L	J	B	A	U	Z	K	A	M	Q
E	S	K	V	D	M	C	S	M	N	V	U
Q	T	U	A	K	J	D	F	G	T	C	A
P	E	A	C	E	F	U	L	R	A	X	L
W	R	G	R	M	T	J	T	D	Z	V	I
S	X	L	A	U	B	O	Y	C	O	T	T
R	D	N	E	K	D	A	C	J	L	R	Y

Martin Luther King Jr. was born in **Atlanta**, Georgia, in 1929.
When Martin graduated from college, he became a **minister**.
Later on, he became a **civil rights** leader.
Martin believed in **peaceful**, or nonviolent, protest.
He led the bus **boycott** in Montgomery, Alabama.
Martin gave his famous "I Have a **Dream**" speech in 1963.
Today, people remember all that he did to fight for **equality**.

74 Just For Fun!

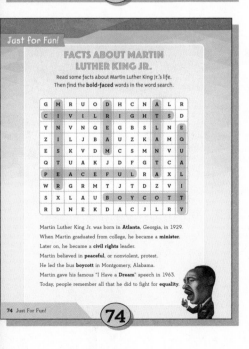

WHAT'S THE QUESTION?

Write the question that goes with each answer. Use the pictures of famous people to help you. The first one has been done for you.

1. **Question:** Who was George Washington?
   Answer: He was a brave general and our country's first president.

2. **Question:** Who was Eleanor Roosevelt?
   Answer: She was the First Lady for 12 years and helped start the United Nations.

3. **Question:** Who was Alexander Hamilton?
   Answer: He was the first secretary of the treasury, and his picture is on the ten-dollar bill.

4. **Question:** Who was Susan B. Anthony?
   Answer: She fought for a woman's right to vote but did not live to see it happen.

5. **Question:** Who was Abraham Lincoln?
   Answer: He was our 16th president and is known as one of our greatest presidents ever.

6. **Question:** Who was Amelia Earhart?
   Answer: She was the first woman to fly solo across the Atlantic Ocean.

7. **Question:** Who was Frederick Douglass?
   Answer: He spoke out against slavery and spent his life fighting for equal rights.

Just For Fun! 75

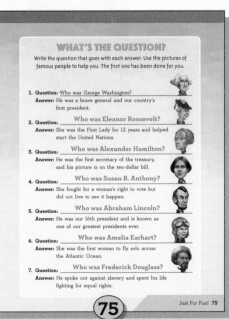

ALL KINDS OF QUESTIONS

Use the passage on the previous page to answer these five questions about Marie Curie.

1. **Where?** Where was Marie born?
   Marie was born in Poland.

2. **Why?** Why did Marie move to France?
   The colleges in Poland didn't allow women, so she moved to France to attend the Sorbonne.

3. **Who?** Who won the Nobel Prize with Marie in 1903?
   Pierre Curie, a French scientist

4. **What?** What metals did Marie discover?
   Marie discovered polonium and radium.

5. **When?** When did Marie win her second Nobel Prize?
   Marie won her second Nobel Prize in 1911.

78 Show What You Know

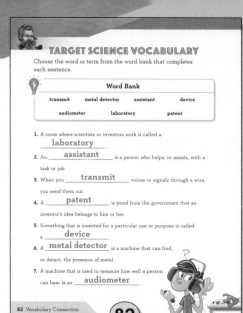

COMPARE AND CONTRAST

How were Marie Curie and Sally Ride alike? How were they different? Write about it on the lines below. You may want to reread the passage about Sally Ride on pages 42-43.

Alike

They were scientists.
They were hard workers.
They became very famous.

Different

Marie lived in France. Sally lived in the U.S. Marie worked in a laboratory. Sally worked in a space shuttle. Marie worked with one partner, Pierre Curie. Sally was part of a crew.

79

TARGET SCIENCE VOCABULARY

Choose the word or term from the word bank that completes each sentence.

Word Bank

transmit   metal detector   assistant   device
audiometer   laboratory   patent

1. A room where scientists or inventors work is called a **laboratory**.
2. An **assistant** is a person who helps, or assists, with a task or job.
3. When you **transmit** voices or signals through a wire, you send them out.
4. A **patent** is proof from the government that an inventor's idea belongs to him or her.
5. Something that is invented for a particular use or purpose is called a **device**.
6. A **metal detector** is a machine that can find, or detect, the presence of metal.
7. A machine that is used to measure how well a person can hear is an **audiometer**.

82

ALEXANDER GRAHAM BELL SUMMARY FRAME

Before I read the passage, I knew **Answers will vary.** about Alexander Graham Bell.

One important thing I learned was _____

_____

I also found out that _____

_____

Another fact I discovered was _____

One fact that surprised me was _____

_____

Some questions that I have about Alexander Graham Bell are:

_____
_____
_____
_____
_____

83

QUESTIONS

1. When did Ulysses S. Grant graduate from West Point Military Academy?
   He graduated from West Point in 1843.

2. Did President Lincoln have confidence in Ulysses S. Grant? Give two facts to support your answer.
   Yes, President Lincoln had confidence in him. He put Ulysses in charge of the entire Union army and gave him the title "lieutenant general."

3. When did the Civil War begin? When did it end?
   The Civil War began in 1861 and ended in 1865.

4. Name one good thing and one bad thing about his presidency.
   Examples: Good – He supported voting rights for Black people. Bad – People who worked for him stole millions of dollars in tax money.

5. When did Ulysses write his memoirs? How old was he when he died?
   He wrote his memoirs in 1885. He was 63 years old when he died.

6. What do you think was Ulysses S. Grant's most important accomplishment? Explain why.
   Answers will vary.

87

Just for Fun!

LAUGH OUT LOUD!

Write the answer to each joke. Use the answer choices in the box on the next page.

What would you get if you crossed the first U.S. president with an animated character?
George Washing-*toon*!

Why did Marie Curie listen to music?
Because she loved *radio*-activity!

What did Johnny Appleseed say when his tree sprouted?
"*Seedling* is believing!"

Why was Amelia Earhart such a great pilot?
Because she had a very positive *altitude*!

Why did Paul Revere ride his horse from Boston to Lexington?
Because the horse was too heavy to carry!

What did Ernest Shackleton say when he first saw penguins in Antarctica?
"Look at those *brrrrrrr*-ds!"

88

Where did Sally Ride leave her spaceship?
At a parking *meteor*!

Why did Davy Crockett wear a crown?
Because he was *King* of the Wild Frontier!

Why did Queen Victoria always measure things?
Because she was a *ruler*!

What did Henry Ford say when he opened his first car factory?
"I'm *wheelie* excited!"

Answer Choices

At a parking *meteor*!
"I'm *wheelie* excited!"
Because the horse was too heavy to carry!
Because she loved *radio*-activity!
George Washing-*toon*!
"Look at those *brrrrrrr*-ds!"
Because he was *King* of the Wild Frontier!
Because she was a *ruler*!
Because she had a very positive *altitude*!
"*Seedling* is believing!"

89